RUDYARD KIPLING

1865-1936

JARROLD POETS SERIES

Other anthologies in this series include:

RUDYARD KIPLING – AN ANTHOLOGY

Poems selected by Joan Forman.
Designed and produced by Parke Sutton Publishing Limited, Norwich
for Jarrold Publishing, Norwich.
First published 1992. Reprinted 1994.

ISBN 0-7117-0400-7

CONTENTS

IF —

("Brother Square-Toes" —
Rewards and Fairies)

If you can keep your head when all about you
   Are losing theirs and blaming it on you,
If you can trust yourself when all men doubt you,
   But make allowance for their doubting too;
If you can wait and not be tired by waiting,
   Or being lied about, don't deal in lies,
Or being hated, don't give way to hating,
   And yet don't look too good, nor talk too wise:

If you can dream — and not make dreams your master;
   If you can think — and not make thoughts your aim;
If you can meet with Triumph and Disaster
   And treat those two impostors just the same;
If you can bear to hear the truth you've spoken
   Twisted by knaves to make a trap for fools,
Or watch the things you gave your life to, broken,
   And stoop and build 'em up with worn-out tools:

If you can make one heap of all your winnings
    And risk it on one turn of pitch-and-toss,
And lose, and start again at your beginnings
    And never breathe a word about your loss;
If you can force your heart and nerve and sinew
    To serve your turn long after they are gone,
And so hold on when there is nothing in you
    Except the Will which says to them: "Hold on!"

If you can talk with crowds and keep your virtue,
    Or walk with Kings — nor lose the common touch,
If neither foes nor loving friends can hurt you,
    If all men count with you, but none too much;
If you can fill the unforgiving minute
    With sixty seconds' worth of distance run,
Yours is the Earth and everything that's in it,
    And — which is more — you'll be a Man, my son!

RECESSIONAL

1897

God of our fathers, known of old,
    Lord of our far-flung battle-line,
Beneath whose awful Hand we hold
    Dominion over palm and pine —
Lord God of Hosts, be with us yet,
Lest we forget — lest we forget!

The tumult and the shouting dies;
    The Captains and the Kings depart:
Still stands Thine ancient sacrifice,
    An humble and a contrite heart.
Lord God of Hosts, be with us yet,
Lest we forget — lest we forget!

Far-called, our navies melt away;
*   On dune and headland sinks the fire:*
Lo, all our pomp of yesterday
*   Is one with Nineveh and Tyre!*
Judge of the Nations, spare us yet,
Lest we forget — lest we forget!

If, drunk with sight of power, we loose
*   Wild tongues that have not Thee in awe,*
Such boastings as the Gentiles use,
*   Or lesser breeds without the Law —*
Lord God of Hosts, be with us yet,
Lest we forget — lest we forget!

For heathen heart that puts her trust
*   In reeking tube and iron shard,*
All valiant dust that builds on dust,
*   And guarding, calls not Thee to guard,*
For frantic boast and foolish word —
Thy mercy on Thy People, Lord!

THE BALLAD OF EAST AND WEST

1889

Oh, East is East, and West is West, and never the
    twain shall meet,
Till Earth and Sky stand presently at God's great
    Judgment Seat;
But there is neither East nor West, Border, nor
    Breed, nor Birth,
When two strong men stand face to face, though
    they come from the ends of the earth!

Kamal is out with twenty men to raise the Border-side,
And he has lifted the Colonel's mare that is the
    Colonel's pride.
He has lifted her out of the stable-door between the dawn
    and the day,
And turned the calkins upon her feet, and ridden her far
    away.
Then up and spoke the Colonel's son that led a troop of
    the Guides:
"Is there never a man of all my men can say where
    Kamal hides?"

Then up and spoke Mohammed Khan, the son of the
  Ressaldar:
"If ye know the track of the morning-mist, ye know
  where his pickets are.
"At dusk he harries the Abazai – at dawn he is into
  Bonair,
"But he must go by Fort Bukloh to his own place to fare.
"So if ye gallop to Fort Bukloh as fast as a bird can fly,
"By the favour of God ye may cut him off ere he win to
  the Tongue of Jagai.
"But if he be past the Tongue of Jagai, right swiftly turn
  ye then,
"For the length and the breadth of that grisly plain is
  sown with Kamal's men.
"There is rock to the left, and rock to the right, and low
  lean thorn between,
"And ye may hear a breech-bolt snick where never a man
  is seen."
The Colonel's son has taken horse, and a raw rough dun
  was he,
With the mouth of a bell and the heart of Hell and the
  head of a gallows-tree.
The Colonel's son to the Fort has won, they bid him stay
  to eat –

Who rides at the tail of a Border thief, he sits not long at his
    meat.
He's up and away from Fort Bukloh as fast as he can fly,
Till he was aware of his father's mare in the gut of the
    Tongue of Jagai,
Till he was aware of his father's mare with Kamal upon her
    back,
And when he could spy the white of her eye, he made the
    pistol crack.
He has fired once, he has fired twice, but the whistling ball
    went wide.
"Ye shoot like a soldier," Kamal said. "Show now if ye can
    ride!"
It's up and over the Tongue of Jagai, as blown dust-devils go,
The dun he fled like a stag of ten, but the mare like a barren
    doe.
The dun he leaned against the bit and slugged his head
    above,
But the red mare played with the snaffle-bars, as a maiden
    plays with a glove.
There was rock to the left and rock to the right, and low lean
    thorn between,
And thrice he heard a breech-bolt snick tho' never a man was
    seen.

11

They have ridden the low moon out of the sky, their hoofs
    drum up the dawn,
The dun he went like a wounded bull, but the mare like a
    new-roused fawn.
The dun he fell at a water-course – in a woeful heap fell he,
And Kamal has turned the red mare back, and pulled the
    rider free.
He has knocked the pistol out of his hand – small room
    was there to strive,
"'Twas only by favour of mine," quoth he, "ye rode so
    long alive:
"There was not a rock for twenty mile, there was not a
    clump of tree,
"But covered a man of my own men with his rifle cocked
    on his knee.
"If I had raised my bridle-hand, as I have held it low,
"The little jackals that flee so fast were feasting all in a row.
"If I had bowed my head on my breast, as I have held it
    high,
"The kite that whistles above us now were gorged till she
    could not fly."
Lightly answered the Colonel's son: "Do good to bird and
    beast,
"But count who come for the broken meats before thou

makest a feast.

"If there should follow a thousand swords to carry my
 bones away,

"Belike the price of a jackal's meal were more than a thief
 could pay.

"They will feed their horse on the standing crop, their
 men on the garnered grain.

"The thatch of the byres will serve their fires when all the
 cattle are slain.

"But if thou thinkest the price be fair, — thy brethren wait
 to sup,

"The hound is kin to the jackal-spawn, — howl, dog, and
 call them up!

"And if thou thinkest the price be high, in steer and gear
 and stack,

"Give me my father's mare again, and I'll fight my own
 way back!"

Kamal has gripped him by the hand and set him upon
 his feet.

"No talk shall be of dogs," said he, "when wolf and grey
 wolf meet.

"May I eat dirt if thou hast hurt of me in deed or breath;

"What dam of lances brought thee forth to jest at the
 dawn with Death?"

Lightly answered the Colonel's son: "I hold by the blood
of my clan:
"Take up the mare for my father's gift — by God, she has
carried a man!"
The red mare ran to the Colonel's son, and nuzzled
against his breast;
"We be two strong men," said Kamal then, "but she
loveth the younger best.
"So she shall go with a lifter's dower, my turquoise-
studded rein,
"My 'broidered saddle and saddle-cloth, and silver
stirrups twain."
The Colonel's son a pistol drew, and held it muzzle-
end,
"Ye have taken the one from a foe," said he. "Will ye
take the mate from a friend?"
"A gift for a gift," said Kamal straight; "a limb for the
risk of a limb.
"Thy father has sent his son to me, I'll send my son to
him!"
With that he whistled his only son, that dropped from a
mountain-crest —
He trod the ling like a buck in spring, and he looked like
a lance in rest.

14

"Now here is thy master," Kamal said, "who leads a troop
    of the Guides,
"And thou must ride at his left side as shield on shoulder
    rides.
"Till Death or I cut loose the tie, at camp and board and
    bed,
"Thy life is his — thy fate it is to guard him with thy head.
"So, thou must eat the White Queen's meat, and all her
    foes are thine,
"And thou must harry thy father's hold for the peace of the
    Border-line,
"And thou must make a trooper tough and hack thy way
    to power —
"Belike they will raise thee to Ressaldar when I am hanged
    in Peshawur!"

They have looked each other between the eyes, and there
    they found no fault.
They have taken the Oath of the Brother-in-Blood on
    leavened bread and salt:
They have taken the Oath of the Brother-in-Blood on fire
    and fresh-cut sod,
On the hilt and the haft of the Khyber knife, and the
    Wondrous Names of God.

15

*The Colonel's son he rides the mare and Kamal's boy
    the dun,*
*And two have come back to Fort Bukloh where there
    went forth but one.*
*And when they drew to the Quarter-Guard, full twenty
    swords flew clear —*
*There was not a man but carried his feud with the blood
    of the mountaineer.*
*"Ha' done! ha' done!" said the Colonel's son. "Put up
    the steel at your sides!*
*"Last night ye had struck at a Border thief — to-night 'tis
    a man of the Guides!"*

Oh, East is East, and West is West, and never the
    twain shall meet,
Till Earth and Sky stand presently at God's great
    Judgment Seat;
But there is neither East nor West, Border, nor
    Breed, nor Birth,
When two strong men stand face to face, though
    they come from the ends of the earth!

ROAD-SONG OF THE BANDAR-LOG

("Kaa's Hunting" – *The Jungle Book*)

Here we go in a flung festoon,
Half-way up to the jealous moon!
Don't you envy our pranceful bands?
Don't you wish you had extra hands?
Wouldn't you like if your tails were – so –
Curved in the shape of a Cupid's bow?
  Now you're angry, but – never mind,
  Brother, thy tail hangs down behind!

Here we sit in a branchy row,
Thinking of beautiful things we know;
Dreaming of deeds that we mean to do,
All complete, in a minute or two –
Something noble and grand and good,
Won by merely wishing we could.
  Now we're going to – never mind,
  Brother, thy tail hangs down behind!

All the talk we ever have heard
Uttered by bat or beast or bird –
Hide or fin or scale or feather –
Jabber it quickly and all together!
Excellent! Wonderful! Once again!
Now we are talking just like men.
   Let's pretend we are ... Never mind!
   Brother, thy tail hangs down behind!
   This is the way of the Monkey-kind!

Then join our leaping lines that scumfish through
the   pines,
That rocket by where, light and high, the wild-
grape   swings.
By the rubbish in our wake, and the noble noise
we   make,
Be sure – be sure, we're going to do some splendid
        things!

THE LAW OF THE JUNGLE

('How Fear Came' – *The Second Jungle Book*)

Now this is the Law of the Jungle – as old and as
  true as the sky;
And the Wolf that shall keep it may prosper, but
  the Wolf that shall break it must die.

As the creeper that girdles the tree-trunk the Law
  runneth forward and back –
For the strength of the Pack is the Wolf, and the
  strength of the Wolf is the Pack.

Wash daily from nose-tip to tail-tip; drink deeply, but
  never too deep;
And remember the night is for hunting, and forget not the
  day is for sleep.

The Jackal may follow the Tiger, but, Cub, when thy
    whiskers are grown,
Remember the Wolf is a hunter — go forth and get food
    of thine own.

Keep peace with the Lords of the Jungle — the Tiger, the
    Panther, the Bear;
And trouble not Hathi the Silent, and mock not the
    Boar in his lair.

When Pack meets with Pack in the Jungle, and neither
    will go from the trail,
Lie down till the leaders have spoken — it may be fair
    words shall prevail.

When ye fight with a Wolf of the Pack, ye must fight
    him alone and afar,
Lest others take part in the quarrel, and the Pack be
    diminished by war.

*The Lair of the Wolf is his refuge, and where he has
    made him his home,
Not even the Head Wolf may enter, not even the
    Council may come.*

*The Lair of the Wolf is his refuge, but where he has
    digged it too plain,
The Council shall send him a message, and so he shall
    change it again.*

*If ye kill before midnight, be silent, and wake not the
    woods with your bay,
Lest ye frighten the deer from the crops, and the brothers
    go empty away.*

*Ye may kill for yourselves, and your mates, and your
    cubs as they need, and ye can;
But kill not for pleasure of killing, and seven times
    never kill Man!*

If ye plunder his Kill from a weaker, devour not all in thy
    pride;
Pack-Right is the right of the meanest; so leave him the
    head and the hide.

The Kill of the Pack is the meat of the Pack. Ye must eat
    where it lies;
And no one may carry away of that meat to his lair, or he
    dies.

The Kill of the Wolf is the meat of the Wolf. He may do
    what he will,
But, till he has given permission, the Pack may not eat of
    that Kill.

Cub-Right is the right of the Yearling. From all of his
    Pack he may claim
Full-gorge when the killer has eaten; and none may refuse
    him the same.

Lair-Right is the right of the Mother. From all of her
    year she may claim
One haunch of each kill for her litter; and none may deny
    her the same.

Cave-Right is the right of the Father — to hunt by
    himself for his own:
He is freed of all calls to the Pack; he is judged by the
    Council alone.

Because of his age and his cunning, because of his gripe
    and his paw,
In all that the Law leaveth open, the word of the head
    Wolf is Law.

Now these are the Laws of the Jungle, and many
    and mighty are they;
But the head and the hoof of the Law and the
    haunch and the hump is — Obey!

GUNGA DIN

You may talk o' gin and beer
When you're quartered safe out 'here,
An' you're sent to penny-fights an' Aldershot it;
But when it comes to slaughter
You will do your work on water,
An' you'll lick the bloomin' boots of 'im that's got it.
Now in Injia's sunny clime,
Where I used to spend my time
A-servin' of 'Er Majesty the Queen,
Of all them blackfaced crew
The finest man I knew
Was our regimental bhisti, Gunga Din.
 He was "Din! Din! Din!
  "You limpin' lump o' brick-dust, Gunga Din!
   "Hi! Slippy hitherao!
   "Water, get it! Panee lao, [1]
  "You squidgy-nosed old idol, Gunga Din."

---

[1] Bring water swiftly.

The uniform 'e wore
Was nothin' much before,
An' rather less than 'arf o' that be'ind,
For a piece o' twisty rag
An' a goatskin water-bag
Was all the field-equipment 'e could find.
When the sweatin' troop-train lay
In a sidin' through the day,
Where the 'eat would make your bloomin' eyebrows crawl,
We shouted "Harry By!" [2]
Till our throats were bricky-dry,
Then we wopped 'im 'cause 'e couldn't serve us all.
    It was "Din! Din! Din!
  "You 'eathen, where the mischief 'ave you been?
    "You put some juldee [3] in it
    "Or I'll marrow [4] you this minute
  "If you don't fill up my helmet, Gunga Din!"

[2] Be quick.

[3] O brother.

[4] Hit you.

25

'E would dot an' carry one
Till the longest day was done;
An' 'e didn't seem to know the use o' fear.
If we charged or broke or cut,
You could bet your bloomin' nut,
'E'd be waitin' fifty paces right flank rear.
With 'is mussick [1] *on is back,*
'E would skip with our attack,
An' watch us till the bugles made "Retire,"
An' for all 'is dirty 'ide
'E was white, clear white, inside
When 'e went to tend the wounded under fire!
    It was "Din! Din! Din!"
    With the bullets kickin' dust-spots on the green.
        When the cartridges ran out,
        You could hear the front-ranks shout,
    "Hi! ammunition-mules an' Gunga Din!"

I shan't forgit the night
When I dropped be'ind the fight
With a bullet where my belt-plate should 'a' been.

[1] Water-skin.

26

I was chokin' mad with thirst,
An' the man that spied me first
Was our good old grinnin', gruntin' Gunga Din.
'E lifted up my 'ead,
An' he plugged me where I bled,
An' 'e guv me 'arf-a-pint o' water green.
It was crawlin' and it stunk,
But of all the drinks I've drunk,
I'm gratefullest to one from Gunga Din.
    It was "Din! Din! Din!
"'Ere's a beggar with a bullet through 'is spleen;
    "'E's chawin' up the ground,
    "An' 'e's kickin' all around:
  "For Gawd's sake git the water, Gunga Din!"

'E carried me away
To where a dooli lay,
An' a bullet come an' drilled the beggar clean.
'E put me safe inside,
An' just before 'e died,
"I 'ope you liked your drink," sez Gunga Din.

So I'll meet 'im later on
At the place where 'e is gone —
Where it's always double drill and no canteen.
'E'll be squattin' on the coals
Givin' drink to poor damned souls,
An' I'll get a swig in hell from Gunga Din!
    Yes, Din! Din! Din!
  You Lazarushian-leather Gunga Din!
    Though I've belted you and flayed you,
    By the livin' Gawd that made you,
    You're a better man than I am, Gunga Din!

THE OVERLAND MAIL

(Foot-service to the Hills)

In the Name of the Empress of India, make way,
   O Lords of the Jungle, wherever you roam,
The woods are astir at the close of the day –
   We exiles are waiting for letters from Home.
Let the robber retreat – let the tiger turn tail –
In the Name of the Empress, the Overland Mail!

With a jingle of bells as the dusk gathers in,
   He turns to the footpath that heads up the hill –
The bags on his back and a cloth round his chin,
   And, tucked in his waistbelt, the Post Office bill:-
"Despatched on this date, as received by the rail,
"Per runner, two bags of the Overland Mail."

Is the torrent in spate? He must ford it or swim.
  Has the rain wrecked the road? He must climb by the
    cliff.
Does the tempest cry halt? What are tempests to him?
  The service admits not a "but" or an "if."
While the breath's in his mouth, he must bear without
    fail,
In the Name of the Empress, the Overland Mail.

From aloe to rose-oak, from rose-oak to fir,
  From level to upland, from upland to crest,
From rice-field to rock-ridge, from rock-ridge to spur,
  Fly the soft-sandalled feet, strains the brawny, brown
    chest.
From rail to ravine — to the peak from the vale —
Up, up through the night goes the Overland Mail.

There's a speck on the hillside, a dot on the road —
  A jingle of bells on the footpath below —
There's a scuffle above in the monkey's abode —
  The world is awake and the clouds are aglow.
For the great Sun himself must attend to the hail:-
  "In the Name of the Empress, the Overland Mail!"

MANDALAY

By the old Moulmein Pagoda, lookin' lazy at the sea,
There's a Burma girl a-settin', and I know she thinks
o' me;
For the wind is in the palm-trees, and the temple-bells
they say:
"Come you back, you British soldier; come you back to
Mandalay!"

Come you back to Mandalay,
Where the old Flotilla lay:
Can't you 'ear their paddles chunkin' from
Rangoon to Mandalay?
On the road to Mandalay,
Where the flyin'-fishes play,
An' the dawn comes up like thunder outer China
'crost the Bay!

'Er petticoat was yaller an' 'er little cap was green,
An' 'er name was Supi-yaw-lat — jes' the same as
Theebaw's Queen,
An' I seed her first a-smokin' of a whackin' white cheroot,
An' a-wastin' Christian kisses on an 'eathen idol's foot:

Bloomin' idol made o' mud –
Wot they called the Great Gawd Budd –
Plucky lot she cared for idols when I kissed 'er
   where she stud!
On the road to Mandalay …

When the mist was on the rice-fields an' the sun was
   droppin' slow,
She'd git 'er little banjo an' she'd sing "Kulla-lo-lo!"
With 'er arm upon my shoulder an' 'er cheek agin my
   cheek
We useter watch the steamers an' the hathis pilin' teak.
   Elephints a-pilin' teak
   In the sludgy, squdgy creek,
   Where the silence 'ung that 'eavy you was 'arf afraid
      to speak!
   On the road to Mandalay …

But that's all shove be'ind me — long ago an' fur away,
An' there ain't no 'buses running' from the Bank to
    Mandalay;
An' I'm learnin' 'ere in London what the ten-year soldier
    tells:
"If you've 'eard the East a-callin', you won't never 'eed
    naught else."
    No! you won't 'eed nothin' else
    But them spicy garlic smells,
    An' the sunshine an' the palm-trees an' the tinkly
       temple-bells;
    On the road to Mandalay …

I am sick o' wastin' leather on these gritty pavin'-stones,
An' the blasted English drizzle wakes the fever in my bones;
Tho' I walks with fifty 'ousemaids outer Chelsea to the
    Strand,
An' they talks a lot o' lovin', but wot do they understand?
    Beefy face an' grubby 'and —
    Law! wot do they understand?
    I've a neater, sweeter maiden in a cleaner, greener
       land!
    On the road to Mandalay…

*Ship me somewheres east of Suez, where the best is like
the worst,*

*Where there aren't no Ten Commandments an' a man
can raise a thirst;*

*For the temple bells are callin', an' it's there that I would
be —*

By the old Moulmein Pagoda, looking lazy at the sea;

    On the road to Mandalay,

    Where the old Flotilla lay,

    *With our sick beneath the awnings when we went
to Mandalay!*

    O the road to Mandalay,

    Where the flyin'-fishes play,

    *An' the dawn comes up like thunder outer China
'crost the Bay!*

THE GIPSY TRAIL

The white moth to the closing bine,
  The bee to the opened clover,
And the gipsy blood to the gipsy blood
  Ever the wide world over.

Ever the wide world over, lass,
  Ever the trail held true,
Over the world and under the world,
  And back at the last to you.

Out of the dark of the gorgio camp,
  Out of the grime and the gray
(Morning waits at the end of the world),
  Gipsy, come away!

The wild boar to the sun-dried swamp,
  The red crane to her reed,
And the Romany lass to the Romany lad
  By the tie of a roving breed.

The pied snake to the rifted rock,
  The buck to the stony plain,
And the Romany lass to the Romany lad,
  And both to the road again.

Both to the road again, again!
  Out on a clean sea-track –
Follow the cross of the gipsy trail
  Over the world and back!

Follow the Romany patteran
  North where the blue bergs sail,
And the bows are gray with the frozen spray,
  And the masts are shod with mail.

Follow the Romany patteran
  Sheer to the Austral Light,
Where the besom of God is the wild South wind,
  Sweeping the sea-floors white.

Follow the Romany patteran
  West to the sinking sun,
Till the junk-sails lift through the houseless drift,
  And the east and the west are one.

Follow the Romany patteran
  East where the silence broods
By a purple wave on an opal beach
  In the hush of the Mahim woods.

'The wild hawk to the wind-swept sky,
  The deer to the wholesome wold,
And the heart of a man to the heart of a maid,
  As it was in the days of old.'

The heart of a man to the heart of a maid —
  Light of my tents, be fleet,
Morning waits at the end of the world,
  And the world is all at our feet!

THE ABSENT-MINDED BEGGAR

When you've shouted "Rule Britannia," when you've
  sung   "God save the Queen,"
    When you've finished killing Kruger with your mouth,
Will you kindly drop a shilling in my little tambourine
    For a gentleman in khaki ordered South?
He's absent-minded beggar, and his weaknesses are great –
    But we and Paul must take him as we find him –
He is out on active service, wiping something off a slate –
    And he's left a lot of little things behind him!
Duke's son – Cook's son – son of a hundred kings –
    (Fifty thousand horse and foot going to Table Bay!)
Each of 'em doing his country's work
    (and who's to look after their things?)
Pass the hat for your credit's sake,
                    and pay – pay – pay!

There are girls he married secret, asking no permission to,
    For he knew he wouldn't get it if he did.
There is gas and coals and vittles, and the house-rent
    falling due,
    And it's more than rather likely there's a kid.

There are girls he walked with casual. They'll be sorry now
      he's gone,
   For an absent-minded beggar they will find him,
But it ain't the time for sermons with the winter coming on.
   We must help the girl that Tommy's left behind him!
Cook's son – Duke's son – son of a belted Earl –
   Son of a Lambeth publican – it's all the same to-day!
Each of 'em doing his country's work
   (and who's to look after the girl?)
Pass the hat for your credit's sake,
                  and pay – pay – pay!

There are families by thousands, far too proud to beg or
      speak,
   And they'll put their sticks and bedding up the spout,
And they'll live on half o' nothing, paid 'em punctual once
      a week,
   'Cause the man that earns the wage is ordered out.
He's an absent-minded beggar, but he heard his country call,
   And his reg'ment didn't need to send to find him!
He chucked his job and joined it – so the job before us all
   Is to help the home that Tommy's left behind him!

Duke's job — cook's job — gardener, baronet, groom,
  Mews or palace or paper-shop, there's someone gone
      away!
Each of 'em doing his country's work
  (and who's to look after the room?)
Pass the hat for your credit's sake,
                and pay — pay — pay!

Let us manage so as, later, we can look him in the face,
  And tell him — what he'd very much prefer —
That, while he saved the Empire, his employer saved his
      place,
  And his mates (that's you and me) looked out for her.
He's an absent-minded beggar and he may forget it all,
  But we do not want his kiddies to remind him
That we sent 'em to the workhouse while their daddy
      hammered Paul,
  So we'll help the homes that Tommy left behind him!
Cook's home — Duke's home — home of a millionaire,
  (Fifty thousand horse and foot going to Table Bay!)
Each of 'em doing his country's work
  (and what have you got to spare?)
Pass the hat for your credit's sake
                and pay — pay — pay!

A Code of Morals

Lest you should think this story true
I merely mention I
Evolved it lately. 'Tis a most
Unmitigated misstatement.

*Now Jones had left his new-wed bride to keep his house
in order,*
*And hied away to the Hurrum Hills above the Afghan
border,*
*To sit on a rock with a heliograph; but ere he left he
taught*
*His wife the working of the Code that sets the miles at
naught.*

*And Love had made him very sage, as Nature made her
fair;*
So Cupid and Apollo linked, per heliograph, the pair.
*At dawn, across the Hurrum Hills, he flashed her counsel
wise —*
At e'en, the dying sunset bore her husband's homilies.

He warned her 'gainst seductive youths in scarlet clad and
    gold,
As much as 'gainst the blandishments paternal of the old;
But kept his gravest warnings for (hereby the ditty hangs)
That snowy-haired Lothario, Lieutenant-General Bangs.

'Twas General Bangs, with Aide and Staff, who
    tittupped on the way,
When they beheld a heliograph tempestuously at play.
They thought of Border risings, and of stations sacked
    and burnt —
So stopped to take the message down — and this is what
    they learnt —

"Dash dot dot, dot, dot dash, dot dash dot" twice. The
    General swore.
"Was ever General Officer addressed as 'dear' before?
"'My Love,' i' faith! 'My Duck,' Gadzooks! 'My
    darling popsy-wop!'
"Spirit of great Lord Wolseley, who is on that
    mountain-top?"

The artless Aide-de-camp was mute, the gilded Staff were
   still,
As, dumb with pent-up mirth, they booked that message
   from the hill;
For clear as summer lightning-flare, the husband's
   warning ran:-
"Don't dance or ride with General Bangs – a most
   immoral man."

[At dawn, across the Hurrum Hills, he flashed her
   counsel wise –
But, howsoever Love be blind, the world at large hath
   eyes.]
With damnatory dot and dash he heliographed his wife
Some interesting details of the General's private life.

The artless Aide-de-camp was mute, the shining Staff
   were still,
And red and ever redder grew the General's shaven gill.
And this is what he said at last (his feelings matter not):-
"I think we've tapped a private line. Hi! Threes about
   there! Trot!"

All honour unto Bangs, for ne'er did Jones thereafter
    know
By word or act official who read off that helio.
But the tale is on the Frontier, and from Michni to
    Mooltan
They know the worthy General as "that most immoral
    man."

"HIS APOLOGIES"

1932

Master, this is Thy Servant. He is rising eight weeks old.
He is mainly Head and Tummy. His legs are
*   uncontrolled.*
But Thou has forgiven his ugliness, and settled him on
*   Thy knee ...*
Art Thou content with Thy Servant? He is very comfy
*   with Thee.*

Master, behold a Sinner! He hath committed a wrong.
He hath defiled Thy Premises through being kept in too
*   long.*
Wherefore his nose has been rubbed in the dirt, and his
*   self-respect has been bruised,*
Master, pardon Thy Sinner, and see he is properly
*   loosèd.*

Master — again Thy Sinner! This that was once Thy
Shoe,
He has found and taken and carried aside, as fitting
matter to chew.
Now there is neither blacking nor tongue, and the
Housemaid has us in tow.
Master, remember Thy Servant is young, and tell her to
let him go!

Master, extol Thy Servant, he has met a most Worthy
Foe!
There has been fighting all over the Shop — and into the
Shop also!
Till cruel umbrellas parted the strife (or I might have been
choking him yet)
But Thy Servant has had the Time of his Life — and
now shall we call on the vet?

Master, behold Thy Servant! Strange children came to
play,
And because they fought to caress him, Thy Servant
wentedst away.
But now that the Little Beasts have gone, he has returned
to see

Master, pity Thy Servant! He is deaf and three parts blind.
He cannot catch Thy Commandments. He cannot read Thy Mind.
Oh, leave him not to his loneliness; nor make him that Kitten's scorn.
He hath had none other God than Thee since the year that he was born.
Lord, look down on Thy Servant! Bad things have come to pass
There is no heat in the mid-day sun, nor health in the wayside grass.
His bones are full of an old disease — his torments run and increase
Lord, make haste with Thy Lightnings and grant him a quick release!

A TRUTHFUL SONG

("The Wrong Thing" – *Rewards and Fairies*)

The Bricklayer:
I tell this tale, which is strictly true,
Just by way of convincing you
How very little, since things were made,
Things have altered in the building trade.

A year ago, come the middle of March,
We was building flats near the Marble Arch,
When a thin young man with coal-black hair
Came up to watch us working there.

Now there wasn't a trick in brick or stone
Which this young man hadn't seen or known;
Nor there wasn't a tool from trowel to maul
But this young man could use 'em all!

Then up and spoke the plumbyers bold,
Which was laying the pipes for the hot and cold:
"Since you with us have made so free,
Will you kindly say what your name might be?"

The young man kindly answered them:
"It might be Lot or Methusalem,
Or it might be Moses (a man I hate),
Whereas it is Pharaoh surnamed the Great.

"Your glazing is new and your plumbing's strange,
But otherwise I perceive no change;
And in less than a month if you do as I bid
I'd learn you to build me a Pyramid!"

The Sailor:
I tell this tale, which is stricter true,
Just by way of convincing you
How very little, since things was made,
Things have altered in the shipwright's trade.

In Blackwall Basin yesterday
A China barque re-fitting lay,
When a fat old man with snow-white hair
Came up to watch us working there.

Now there wasn't a knot which the riggers knew
But the old man made it — and better too;
Nor there wasn't a sheet, or a lift, or a brace,
But the old man knew its lead and place.

Then up and spoke the caulkyers bold,
Which was packing the pump in the afterhold:
"Since you with us have made so free,
Will you kindly tell what your name might be?"

The old man kindly answered them:
"It might be Japheth, it might be Shem,
Or it might be Ham (though his skin was dark),
Whereas it is Noah, commanding the Ark."

"Your wheel is new and your pumps are strange,
But otherwise I perceive no change;
And in less than a week, if she did not ground,
I'd sail this hooker the wide world round!"

Both
We tell these tales, which are strictest true,
Just by way of convincing you
How very little, since things was made,
Anything alters in any one's trade!

THE 'MARY GLOSTER'

1894

*I've paid for your sickest fancies; I've humoured your
  crackedest whim —*
Dick, it's your daddy, dying; you've got to listen to him!
Good for a fortnight, am I? The doctor told you? He lied.
I shall go under by morning, and — Put that nurse outside.
*'Never seen death yet, Dickie? Well, now is your time to
  learn,*
*And you'll wish you held my record before it comes to your
  turn.*
*Not counting the Line and the Foundry, the Yards and the
  village, too,*
*I've made myself and a million; but I'm damned if I made
  you.*
Master at two-and-twenty, and married at twenty-three —
*Ten thousand men on the pay-roll, and forty freighters at
  sea!*
Fifty years between 'em, and every year of it fight,
And now I'm Sir Anthony Gloster, dying a baronite:
*For I lunched with his Royal 'Ighness — what was it the
  papers had?*

'Not least of our merchant-princes.' Dickie, that's me, your
    dad!
I didn't begin with askings. I took my job and I stuck;
I took the chances they wouldn't, an' now they're calling it
    luck.
Lord, what boats I've handled — rotten and leaky and old —
Ran 'em or — opened the bilge-cock, precisely as I was told
Grub that 'ud bind you crazy, and crews that 'ud turn you
    grey,
And a big fat lump of insurance to cover the risk on the
    way.
The others they dursn't do it; they said they valued their life
(They've served me since as skippers). I went, and I took
    my wife.
Over the world I drove 'em, married at twenty-three,
And your mother saving money and making a man of me.
I was content to be master, but she said there was better
    behind;
She took the chances I wouldn't, and I followed your mother
    blind.
She egged me to borrow the money, an' she helped me to
    clear the loan,
When we bought half-shares in a cheap 'un and hoisted a
    flag of our own.

Patching and coaling on credit, and living the Lord knew
how,

We started the Red Ox freighters — we've eight-and-thirty
now.

And those were the days of clippers, and the freights were
clipper-freights,

And we knew we were making our fortune, but she died in
Macassar Straits —

By the Little Paternosters, as you come to the Union Bank —

And we dropped her in fourteen fathom: I pricked it off
where she sank.

Owners we were, full owners, and the boat was christened
for her,

And she died in the Mary Gloster. My heart, how young
we were!

So I went on a spree round Java and wellnigh ran her
ashore,

But your mother came and warned me and I wouldn't
liquor no more:

Strict I stuck to my business, afraid to stop or I'd think,

Saving the money (she warned me), and letting the other
men drink.

And I met M'Cullough in London (I'd saved five 'undred
then),

And 'tween us we started the Foundry — three forges and
  twenty men.
Cheap repairs for the cheap 'uns. It paid, and the
  business grew;
For I bought me a steam-lathe patent, and that was a
  gold mine too.
'Cheaper to build 'em than buy 'em,' I said, but
  M'Cullough he shied,
And we wasted a year in talking before we moved to the
  Clyde.
And the Lines were all beginning, and we all of us started
  fair,
Building our engines like houses and staying the boilers
  square.
But M'Cullough 'e wanted cabins with marble and
  maple and all,
And Brussels an' Utrecht velvet, and baths and a Social
  Hall,
And pipes for closets all over, and cutting the frames too
  light,
But M'Cullough he died in the Sixties, and — Well, I'm
  dying to-night ...
I knew — I knew what was coming, when we bid on the
  Byfleet's keel —

They piddled and piffled with iron. I'd given my orders
  for steel!
Steel and the first expansions. It paid, I tell you, it paid,
When we came with our nine-knot freighters and collared
  the long-run trade!
And they asked me how I did it, and I gave 'em the
  Scripture text,
'You keep your light so shining a little in front o' the
  next!'
They copied all they could follow, but they couldn't copy
  my mind,
And I left 'em sweating and stealing a year and a half
  behind.
Then came the armour-contracts, but that was
  M'Cullough's side;
He was always best in the Foundry, but better, perhaps,
  he died.
I went through his private papers; the notes was plainer
  than print;
And I'm no fool to finish if a man'll give me a hint.
(I remember his widow was angry.) So I saw what his
  drawings meant,
And I started with six-inch rollers, and it paid me sixty
  per cent.

Sixty per cent with failures, and more than twice we could do,
And a quarter-million to credit, and I saved it all for you!
I thought — it doesn't matter — you seemed to favour your ma,
But you're nearer forty than thirty, and I know the kind you are.
Harrer an' Trinity College! I ought to ha' sent you to sea —
But I stood you an education, an' what have you done for me?
The things I knew was proper you wouldn't thank me to give,
And the things I knew was rotten you said was the way to live.
For you muddled with books and pictures, an' china an' etchin's an' fans,
And your rooms at college was beastly — more like a whore's than a man's;
Till you married that thin-flanked woman, as white and as stale as a bone,
An' she gave you your social nonsense; but where's that kid o' your own?
I've seen your carriages blocking the half o' the Cromwell Road,

But never the doctor's brougham to help the missus unload.
(So there isn't even a grandchild, an' the Gloster family's done.)
Not like your mother, she isn't. She carried her freight each run.
But they died, the pore little beggars! At sea she had 'em — they died.
Only you, an' you stood it. You haven't stood much beside.
Weak, a liar, and idle, and mean as a collier's whelp
Nosing for scraps in the galley. No help — my son was no help!
So he gets three 'undred thousand, in trust and the interest paid.
I wouldn't give it you, Dickie — you see, I made it in trade.
You're saved from soiling your fingers, and if you have no child,
It all comes back to the business. 'Gad, won't your wife be wild!
'Calls and calls in her carriage, her 'andkerchief up to 'er eye:
'Daddy, dear daddy's dyin'!' and doing her best to cry.
Grateful? Oh, yes, I'm grateful, but keep her away from here.

Your mother 'ud never ha' stood 'er, and, anyhow,
  women are queer ...
There's women will say I've married a second time. Not
  quite!
But give pore Aggie a hundred, and tell her your
  lawyers'll fight.
She was the best o' the boiling – you'll meet her before it
  ends.
I'm in for a row with the mother – I'll leave you settle
  my friends.
For a man he must go with a woman, which women
  don't understand –
Or the sort that say they can see it they aren't the
  marrying brand.
But I wanted to speak o' your mother that's Lady
  Gloster still;
I'm going to up and see her, without its hurting the will.
Here! Take your hand off the bell-pull. Five thousand's
  waiting for you,
If you'll only listen a minute, and do as I bid you do.
They'll try to prove me crazy, and, if you bungle, they
  can;
And I've only you to trust to! (O God, why ain't it a
  man?)

There's some waste money on marbles, the same as
    M'Cullough tried –
Marbles and mausoleums – but I call that sinful pride.
There's some ship bodies for burial – we've carried 'em,
    soldered and packed;
Down in their wills they wrote it, and nobody called them
    cracked.
But me – I've too much money, and people might ... All
    my fault:
It come o' hoping for grandsons and buying that Wokin'
    vault ...
I'm sick o' the 'ole dam' business. I'm going back where I
    came.
Dick, you're the son o' my body, and you'll take charge o'
    the same!
I want to lie by your mother, ten thousand mile away,
And they'll want to send me to Woking; and that's where
    you'll earn your pay.
I've thought it out on the quiet, the same as it ought to be
    done –
Quiet, and decent, and proper – an' here's your orders, my
    son.
You know the Line? You don't, though. You write to the
    Board, and tell

Your father's death has upset you an' you're goin' to cruise
for a spell,
An' you'd like the Mary Gloster — I've held her ready for
this —
They'll put her in working order and you'll take her out as
she is.
Yes, it was money idle when I patched her and laid her
aside
(Thank God, I can pay for my fancies!) — the boat where
your mother died,
By the Little Paternosters, as you come to the Union Bank,
We dropped her — I think I told you — and I pricked it off
where she sank.
['Tiny she looked on the grating — that oily treacly sea —]
'Hundred and Eighteen East, remember, and South just
Three.
Easy bearings to carry — Three South — Three to the dot;
But I gave McAndrew a copy in case of dying — or not.
And so you'll write to McAndrew, he's Chief of the Maori
Line;
They'll give him leave, if you ask 'em and say it's business o'
mine.
I built three boats for the Maoris, an' very well pleased they
were,

61

An' I've known Mac since the fifties, and Mac knew me —
*   and her.*
After the first stroke warned me I sent him the money to keep
Against the time you'd claim it, committin' your dad to the
*   deep;*
For you are the son o' my body, and Mac was my oldest
*   friend,*
I've never asked 'im to dinner, but he'll see it out to the end.
Stiff-necked Glasgow beggar! I've heard he's prayed for my
*   soul,*
But he couldn't lie if you paid him, and he'd starve before he
*   stole.*
He'll take the Mary in ballast — You'll find her a lively
*   ship;*
And you'll take Sir Anthony Gloster, that goes on 'is
*   wedding-trip,*
Lashed in our old deck-cabin with all three port-holes wide,
The kick o' the screw beneath him and the round blue seas
*   outside!*
Sir Anthony Gloster's carriage — our 'ouse-flag flyin' free —
Ten thousand men on the pay-roll and forty freighters at sea!
He made himself and a million, but this world is a fleetin'
*   show,*
And he'll go to the wife of 'is bosom the same as he ought to
*   go —*

By the heel of the Paternosters – there isn't a chance to
mistake –
And Mac'll pay you the money as soon as the bubbles
break!
Five thousand for six weeks' cruising, the staunchest
freighter afloat,
And Mac he'll give you your bonus the minute I'm out
o' the boat!
He'll take you round to Macassar, and you'll come back
alone;
He knows what I want o' the Mary ... I'll do what I
please with my own.
Your mother 'ud call it wasteful, but I've seven-and-
thirty more;
I'll come in my private carriage and bid it wait at the
door ...
For my son 'e was never a credit: 'e muddled with books
and art,
And 'e lived on Sir Anthony's money and 'e broke Sir
Anthony's heart.
There isn't even a grandchild, and the Gloster family's
done –
The only one you left me – O mother, the only one!

Harrer and Trinity College — me slavin' early an' late —
An' he thinks I'm dying crazy, and you're in Macassar Strait!
Flesh o' my flesh, my dearie, for ever an' ever amen,
That first stroke come for a warning. I ought to ha' gone to you then.
But — cheap repairs for a cheap 'un — the doctors said I'd do.
Mary, why didn't you warn me? I've allus heeded to you,
Excep' — I know — about women; but you are a spirit now;
An', wife, they was only woman, and I was a man. That's how.
An' a man 'e must go with a woman, as you could not understand;
But I never talked 'em secrets. I paid 'em out o' hand.
Thank Gawd, I can pay for my fancies! Now what's five thousand to me,
For a berth off the Paternosters in the haven where I would be?
I believe in the Resurrection, if I read my Bible plain,
But I wouldn't trust 'em at Wokin'; we're safer at sea again.

For the heart it shall go with the treasure — go down to
  the sea in ships.
I'm sick of the hired women. I'll kiss my girl on her lips!
I'll be content with my fountain. I'll drink from my own
  well,
And the wife of my youth shall charm me — an' the rest
  can go to Hell!
(Dickie, he will, that's certain.) I'll lie in our standin'-
  bed,
An' Mac'll take her in ballast — an' she trims best by the
  head ...
Down by the head an' sinkin', her fires are drawn and
  cold,
And the water's splashin' hollow on the skin of the
  empty hold —
Churning an' choking and chuckling, quiet and scummy
  and dark —
Full to her lower hatches and risin' steady. Hark!
That was the after-bulkhead ... She's flooded from stem
  to stern ...
'Never seen death yet, Dickie? ... Well, now is your
  time to learn!

DELILAH

We have another Viceroy now, — those days are
dead and done
Of Delilah Aberyswith and depraved Ulysses Gunne.

Delilah Aberyswith was a lady — not too young —
With a perfect taste in dresses and a badly-bitted tongue,
With a thirst for information, and a greater thirst for
praise,
And a little house in Simla in the Prehistoric Days.

By reason of her marriage to a gentleman in power,
Delilah was acquainted with the gossip of the hour;
And many little secrets, of the half-official kind,
Were whispered to Delilah, and she bore them all in
mind.

She patronised extensively a man, Ulysses Gunne,
Whose mode of earning money was a low and shameful
one.
He wrote for certain papers, which, as everybody knows,
Is worse than serving in a shop or scaring off the crows.

He praised her "queenly beauty" first; and, later on, he hinted
At the "vastness of her intellect" with compliment un-
stinted.
He went with her a-riding, and his love for her was such
That he lent her all his horses and — she galled them very
much.

One day, They brewed a secret of a fine financial sort;
It related to Appointments, to a Man and a Report.
'Twas almost worth the keepin', — only seven people knew
it —
And Gunne rose up to seek the truth and patiently ensue it.

It was a Viceroy's Secret, but — perhaps the wine was red —
Perhaps an Aged Councillor had lost his aged head —
Perhaps Delilah's eyes were bright — Delilah's whispers
sweet —
The Aged Member told her what 'twere treason to repeat.

Ulysses went a-riding, and they talked of love and flowers,
Ulysses went a-calling, and he called for several hours;
Ulysses went a-waltzing, and Delilah helped him dance —
Ulysses let the waltzes go, and waited for his chance.

The summer sun was setting, and the summer air was
   still,
The couple went a-walking in the shade of Summer Hill.
The wasteful sunset faded out in turkis-green and gold,
Ulysses pleaded softly, and ... that bad Delilah told!

Next morn, a startled Empire learnt the all-important
   news;
Next week, the Aged Councillor was shaking in his
   shoes.
Next month, I met Delilah and she did not show the
   least
Hesitation in affirming that Ulysses was a "beast."

We have another Viceroy now, those days are dead and
   done —
Off, Delilah Aberyswith and most mean Ulysses Gunne!

THE LADIES

I've taken my fun where I've found it;
  I've rogued an' I've ranged in my time;
I've 'ad my pickin' o' sweethearts,
  An four o' the lot was prime.
One was an 'arf-caste widow,
  One was a woman at Prome,
One was the wife of a jemadar-sais,
  An' one is a girl at 'ome.

Now I aren't no 'and with the ladies,
  For, takin' 'em all along,
You never can say till you've tried 'em,
  An' then you are like to be wrong.
There's times when you'll think that you mightn't,
  There's times when you'll know that you might;
But the things you will learn from the Yellow an'
    Brown,
  They'll 'elp you a lot with the White!

I was a young un at 'Oogli,
   Shy as a girl to begin;
Aggie de Castrer she made me,
   An' Aggie was clever as sin;
Older than me, but my first un –
   More like a mother she were –
Showed me the way to promotion an' pay,
   An' I learned about women from 'er!

Then I was ordered to Burma,
   Actin' in charge o' Bazar,
An' I got me a tiddy live 'eathen
   Through buyin' supplies off 'er pa.
Funny an' yellow an' faithful –
   Doll in a teacup she were –
But we lived on the square, like a true-married pair,
   An' I learned about women from 'er!

Then we was shifted to Neemuch
    (Or I might ha' been keepin' 'er now),
An' I took with a shiny she-devil,
    The wife of a nigger at Mhow;
'Taught me the gipsy-folks' bolee; [1]
    Kind o' volcano she were,
For she knifed me one night 'cause I wished she was
        white,
    And I learned about women from 'er!

Then I come 'ome in a trooper,
    'Long of a kid o' sixteen —
'Girl from a convent at Meerut,
    The straightest I ever 'ave seen.
Love at first sight was 'er trouble,
    She *didn't* know what it were;
An' I wouldn't do such, 'cause I liked 'er too much,
    But — I learned about women from 'er!

[1] Slang

I've taken my fun where I've found it,
   An' now I must pay for my fun,
For the more you 'ave known o' the others
   The less will you settle to one;
An' the end of it's sittin' and thinkin',
   An' dreamin' Hell-fires to see;
So be warned by my lot (which I know you will not),
   An' learn about women from me!

What did the Colonel's Lady think?
   Nobody never knew.
Somebody asked the Sergeant's Wife,
   An' she told 'em true!
When you get to a man in the case,
   They're like as a row of pins –
For the Colonel's Lady an' Judy O'Grady
   Are sisters under their skins!

GENTLEMEN-RANKERS

To the legion of the lost ones, to the cohort of the
   damned,
   To my brethren in their sorrow overseas,
Sings a gentleman of England cleanly bred, machinely
   crammed,
   And a trooper of the Empress, if you please.
Yes, a trooper of the forces who has run his own six
   horses,
   And faith he went the pace and went it blind,
And the world was more than kin while he held the ready
   tin,
   But to-day the Sergeant's something less than kind.
      We're poor little lambs who've lost our way,
         Baa! Baa! Baa!
      We're little black sheep who've gone astray,
         Baa — aa — aa!
      Gentlemen-rankers out on the spree,
      Damned from here to Eternity,
      God ha' mercy on such as we,
         Baa! Yah! Bah!

Oh, it's sweet to sweat through stables, sweet to empty
    kitchen slops,
    And it's sweet to hear the tales the troopers tell,
To dance with blowzy housemaids at the regimental hops
    And thrash the cad who says you waltz too well.
Yes, it makes you cock-a-hoop to be 'Rider' to your
    troop,
    And branded with a blasted worsted spur,
When you envy, O how keenly, one poor Tommy living
    cleanly
    Who blacks your boots and sometimes calls you 'Sir'.

If the home we never write to, and the oaths we never
    keep,
    And all we know most distant and most dear,
Across the snoring barrack-room return to break our sleep,
    Can you blame us if we soak ourselves in beer?
When the drunken comrade mutters and the great guard-
    lantern gutters
    And the horror of our fall is written plain,
Every secret, self-revealing on the aching whitewashed
    ceiling,
    Do you wonder that we drug ourselves from pain?

We have done with Hope and Honour, we are lost to
     Love and Truth,
  We are dropping down the ladder rung by rung,
And the measure of our torment is the measure of our
     youth.
  God help us, for we knew the worst too young!
Our shame is clean repentance for the crime that brought
     the sentence,
  Our pride it is to know no spur of pride,
And the Curse of Reuben holds us till an alien turf
     enfolds us
  And we die, and none can tell Them where we died.

          We're poor little lambs who've lost our way,
               Baa! Baa! Baa!
          We're little black sheep who've gone astray,
               Baa − aa − aa!
          Gentlemen-rankers out on the spree,
          Damned from here to Eternity,
          God Ha' mercy on such as we,
               Baa! Yah! Bah!

MY RIVAL

I go to concert, party, ball —
  What profit is in these?
I sit alone against the wall
  And strive to look at ease.
The incense that is mine by right
  They burn before Her shrine;
And that's because I'm seventeen
  And she is forty-nine.

I cannot check my girlish blush,
  My colour comes and goes.
I redden to my finger-tips,
  And sometimes to my nose.
But She is white where white should be,
  And red where red should shine.
The blush that flies at seventeen
  Is fixed at forty-nine.

I wish I had her constant cheek:
   I wish that I could sing
All sorts of funny little songs,
   Not quite the proper thing.
I'm very gauche and very shy,
   Her jokes aren't in my line;
And, worst of all, I'm seventeen
   While She is forty-nine.

The young men come, the young men go,
   Each pink and white and neat,
She's older than their mothers, but
   They grovel at Her feet.
They walk beside Her rickshaw-wheels —
   None ever walk by mine;
And that's because I'm seventeen
   And She is forty-nine.

She rides with half a dozen men
   (She calls them "boys" and "mashes"),
I trot along the Mall alone;
   My prettiest frocks and sashes

Don't help to fill my programme-card,
    And vainly I repine
From ten to two A.M. Ah me!
    Would I were forty-nine.

She calls me "darling," "pet," and "dear,"
    And "sweet retiring maid."
I'm always at the back, I know —
    She puts me in the shade.
She introduces me to men —
    "Cast" lovers, I opine;
For sixty takes to seventeen,
    Nineteen to forty-nine.

But even She must older grow
    And end Her dancing days,
She can't go on for ever so
    At concerts, balls, and plays.
One ray of priceless hope I see
    Before my footsteps shine;
Just think, that She'll be eighty-one
    When I am forty-nine!

FOX-HUNTING

(The Fox Meditates)

1933

When Samson set my brush afire
    To spoil the Timnites' barley,
I made my point for Leicestershire
    And left Philistia early.
Through Gath and Rankesborough Gorse I fled,
    And took the Coplow Road, sir!
And was a Gentleman in Red
    When all the Quorn wore woad, sir!

When Rome lay massed on Hadrian's Wall,
    And nothing much was doing,
Her bored Centurions heard my call
    O'nights when I went wooing.
They raised a pack – they ran it well
    (For I was there to run 'em)
From Aesica to Carter Fell,
    And down North Tyne to Hunnum.

When William landed hot for blood,
   And Harold's hosts were smitten,
I lay at earth in battle Wood
   While Domesday Book was written.
Whatever harm he did to man,
   I owe him pure affection;
For in his righteous reign began
   The first of Game Protection.

When Charles, my namesake, lost his mask,
   And Oliver dropped his'n,
I found those Northern Squires a task,
   To keep 'em out of prison.
In boots as big as milking-pails,
   With holsters on the pommel,
They chevied me across the Dales
   Instead of fighting Cromwell.

When thrifty Walpole took the helm,
   And hedging came in fashion,
The March of Progress gave my realm
   Enclosure and Plantation.

'Twas then, to soothe their discontent,
  I showed each pounded Master,
However fast the Commons went,
  I went a little faster!

When Pigg and Jorrocks held the stage,
  And Steam had linked the Shires,
I broke the staid Victorian age
  To posts, and rails, and wires.
Then fifty mile was none too far
  To go by train to cover,
Till some dam' sutler pupped a car,
  And decent sport was over!

When men grew shy of hunting stag,
  For fear the Law might try 'em,
The Car put up an average bag
  Of twenty dead per diem.
Then every road was made a rink
  For Coroners to sit on;
And so began, in skid and stink,
  The real blood-sport of Britain!

THE WAY THROUGH THE WOODS

("Marklake Witches" – *Rewards and Fairies*)

They shut the road through the woods
Seventy years ago.
Weather and rain have undone it again,
And now you would never know
There was once a road through the woods
Before they planted the trees.
It is underneath the coppice and heath
And the thin anemones.
Only the keeper sees
That, where the ring dove broods,
And the badgers roll at ease,
There was once a road through the woods.

Yet, if you enter the woods
Of a summer evening late,
When the night-air cools on the trout-ringed pools
Where the otter whistles his mate,
(They fear not men in the woods,
Because they see so few.)
You will hear the beat of a horse's feet,
And the swish of a skirt in the dew,
Steadily cantering through
The misty solitudes,
As though they perfectly knew
The old lost road through the woods ...
But there is no road through the woods.

In Springtime

My garden blazes brightly with the rose-bush and
    the peach,
  And the koïl sings above it, in the siris by the well,
From the creeper-covered trellis comes the squirrel's
    chattering speech,
  And the blue jay screams and flutters where the cheery
    sat-bhai dwell.
But the rose has lost its fragrance, and the koïl's note is
    strange;
  I am sick of endless sunshine, sick of blossom-burdened
    bough.
Give me back the leafless woodlands where the winds of
    Springtime range –
  Give me back one day in England, for it's Spring in
    England now!

Through the pines the gusts are booming, o'er the brown
    fields blowing chill,
  From the furrow of the ploughshare streams the fragrance
    of the loam,
And the hawk nests on the cliffside and the jackdaw in the
    hill,

And my heart is back in England 'mid the sights and
   sounds of Home.
But the garland of the sacrifice this wealth of rose and
   peach is
Ah! koïl, *little* koïl, *singing on the* siris *bough,*
In my ears the knell of exile your ceaseless bell like speech
   is —
   Can you tell me aught of England or of Spring in
      England now?

THE GLORY OF THE GARDEN

Our England is a garden that is full of stately views,
Of borders, beds and shrubberies and lawns and avenues,
With statues on the terraces and peacocks strutting by;
But the Glory of the Garden lies in more than meets the
*   eye.*

For where the old thick laurels grow, along the thin red
*   wall,*
You find the tool- and potting-sheds which are the heart
*   of all;*
The cold-frames and the hot-houses, the dungpits and the
*   tanks,*
The rollers, carts and drain-pipes, with the barrows and
*   the planks.*

And there you'll see the gardeners, the men and 'prentice
*   boys*
Told off to do as they are bid and do it without noise;
For, except when seeds are planted and we shout to scare
*   the birds,*
The Glory of the Garden it abideth not in words.

And some can pot begonias and some can bud a rose,

And some are hardly fit to trust with anything that grows;

But they can roll and trim the lawns and sift the sand and loam,

For the Glory of the Garden occupieth all who come.

Our England is a garden, and such gardens are not made

By singing: - "Oh, how beautiful!" and sitting in the shade,

While better men than we go out and start their working lives

At grubbing weeds from gravel-paths with broken dinner-knives.

There's not a pair of legs so thin, there's not a head so thick,

There's not a hand so weak and white, nor yet a heart so sick,

But it can find some needful job that's crying to be done,

For the Glory of the Garden glorifieth every one.

Then seek your job with thankfulness and work till
  further orders,
If it's only netting strawberries or killing slugs on borders;
And when your back stops aching and your hands begin
  to harden,
You will find yourself a partner in the Glory of the
  Garden.

Oh, Adam was a gardener, and God who made him
  sees
That half a proper gardener's work is done upon his
  knees,
So when your work is finished, you can wash your hands
  and pray
For the Glory of the Garden, that it may not pass away!
And the glory of the Garden it shall never pass
  away!

THE LAND

When Julius Fabricius, Sub-Prefect of the Weald,
In the days of Diocletian owned our Lower River-field,
He called to him Hobdenius — a Briton of the Clay,
Saying: "What about that River-piece for layin' in to
hay?"

And the aged Hobden answered: "I remember as a lad
My father told your father that she wanted dreenin' bad.
An' the more that you neeglect her the less you'll get her
clean.
Have it jest as you've a mind to, but, if I was you, I'd
dreen."

So they drained it long and crossways in the lavish
Roman style —
Still we find among the river-drift their flakes of ancient
tile,
And in drouthy middle August, when the bones of
meadows show,
We can trace the lines they followed sixteen hundred
years ago.

Then Julius Fabricius died as even Prefects do,
And after certain centuries, Imperial Rome died too.
Then did robbers enter Britain from across the Northern
  main
And our Lower River-field was won by Ogier the Dane.

Well could Ogier work his war-boat – well could Ogier
  wield his brand –
Much he knew of foaming waters – not so much of
  farming land.
So he called to him a Hobden of the old unaltered blood,
Saying: "What about that River-piece? she doesn't look
  no good."

And that aged Hobden answered: "'Tain't for me to
  interfere,
But I've known that bit o' meadow now for five and fifty
  year.
Have it jest as you've a mind to, but I've proved it time
  on time,
If you want to change her nature you have got to give her
  lime!"

Ogier sent his wains to Lewes, twenty hours' solemn walk,
And drew back great abundance of the cool, grey, healing
  chalk.

90

And old Hobden spread it broadcast, never heeding what
   was in't. —
Which is why in cleaning ditches, now and then we find a
   flint.

Ogier died. His sons grew English — Anglo-Saxon was
   their name —
Till out of blossomed Normandy another pirate came;
For Duke William conquered England and divided with
   his men,
And our Lower River-field he gave to William of
   Warenne.

But the Brook (you know her habit) rose one rainy autumn
   night
And tore down sodden flitches of the bank to left and right.
So, said William to his Bailiff as they rode their dripping
   rounds:
"Hob, what about that River-bit — the Brook's got up no
   bounds?"

And that aged Hobden answered: "'Tain't my business to
   advise,
But ye might ha' known 'twould happen from the way the
   valley lies.

Where ye can't hold back the water you must try and save
    the sile.
Hev it jest as you've a mind to, but, if I was you, I'd
    spile!"

They spiled along the water-course with trunks of willow-
    trees,
And planks of elms behind 'em and immortal oaken knees.
And when the spates of Autumn whirl the gravel-beds
    away
You can see their faithful fragments, iron-hard in iron clay.

Georgii Quinti Anno Sexto, I, who own the River-
    field,
Am fortified with title-deeds, attested, signed and sealed,
    Guaranteeing me, my assigns, my executors and heirs
All sorts of powers and profits which — are neither mine nor
    theirs.

I have rights of chase and warren, as my dignity requires.
I can fish — but Hobden tickles. I can shoot — but Hobden
    wires.
I repair, but he reopens, certain gaps which, men allege,
Have been used by every Hobden since a Hobden swapped
    a hedge.

Shall I dog his morning progress o'er the track-betraying dew?
Demand his dinner-basket into which my pheasant flew?
Confiscate his evening faggot under which my conies ran,
And summons him to judgment? I would sooner summons
    Pan.

His dead are in the churchyard — thirty generations laid.
Their names were old in history when Domesday Book was
    made;
And the passion and the piety and prowess of his line
Have seeded, rooted, fruited in some land the Law calls
    mine.

Not for any beast that burrows, not for any bird that flies,
Would I lose his large sound counsel, miss his keen
    amending eyes.
He is bailiff, woodman, wheelwright, field-surveyor,
    engineer,
And if flagrantly a poacher — 'tain't for me to interfere.

"Hob, what about that River-bit" I turn to him again,
With Fabricius and Ogier and William of Warenne.
"Hev it jest as you've a mind to, but" — and here he takes
    command.
For whoever pays the taxes old Mus' Hobden owns the land.

THE RIVER'S TALE

(Prehistoric)

Twenty bridges from Tower to Kew —
(Twenty bridges or twenty-two) —
Wanted to know what the River knew,
For they were young and the Thames was old,
And this is the tale that the River told :-

"I walk my beat before London Town,
Five hours up and seven down.
Up I go till I end my run
At Tide-end-town, which is Teddington.
Down I come with the mud in my hands
And plaster it over the Maplin Sands.
But I'd have you know that these waters of mine
Were once a branch of the River Rhine,
When hundreds of miles to the East I went
And England was joined to the Continent.

I remember the bat-winged lizard-birds,
The Age of Ice and the mammoth herds,
And the giant tigers that stalked them down
Through Regent's Park into Camden Town.

And I remember like yesterday
The earliest Cockney who came my way,
When he pushed through the forest that lined the Strand,
With paint on his face and a club in his hand.
He was death to feather and fin and fur.
He trapped my beavers at Westminster.
He netted my salmon, he hunted my deer,
He killed my heron off Lambeth Pier.
He fought his neighbour with axes and swords,
Flint or bronze, at my upper fords,
While down at Greenwich, for slaves and tin,
The tall Phoenician ships stole in,
And North Sea war-boats, painted and gay,
Flashed like dragon-flies, Erith way;
And Norseman and Negro and Gaul and Greek
Drank with the Britons in Barking Creek,

And life was gay, and the world was new,
And I was a mile across at Kew!
But the Roman came with a heavy hand,
And bridged and roaded and ruled the land,
And the Roman left and the Danes blew in –
And that's where your history-books begin!"

A SMUGGLER'S SONG

("Hal o' the Draft" – *Puck of Pook's Hill*)

If you wake at midnight, and hear a horse's feet,
Don't go drawing back the blind, or looking in the street,
Them that asks no questions isn't told a lie.
Watch the wall, my darling, while the Gentlemen go by!
   Five and twenty ponies
   Trotting through the dark –
   Brandy for the Parson,
   'Baccy for the Clerk;
Laces for a lady, letters for a spy,
And watch the wall, my darling, while the Gentlemen go
   by!

Running round the woodlump if you chance to find
Little barrels, roped and tarred, all full of brandy-wine,
Don't you shout to come and look, nor use 'em for your
   play.
Put the brishwood back again – and they'll be gone next
   day!

If you see the stable-door setting open wide;
If you see a tired horse lying down inside;
If your mother mends a coat cut about and tore;
If the lining's wet and warm — don't you ask no more!

If you meet King George's men, dressed in blue and red,
You be careful what you say, and mindful what is said.
If they call you "pretty maid," and chuck you 'neath the
    chin,
Don't you tell where no one is, nor yet where no one's
    been!

Knocks and footsteps round the house — whistles after
    dark —
You've no call for running out till the house-dogs bark.
Trusty's here, and Pincher's here, and see how dumb
    they lie —
They don't fret to follow when the Gentlemen go by!

If you do as you've been told, 'likely there's a chance,
You'll be give a dainty doll, all the way from France,
With a cap of Valenciennes, and a velvet hood —
A present from the Gentlemen, along o' being good!
    Five and twenty ponies
    Trotting through the dark —
    Brandy for the Parson,
    'Baccy for the Clerk.
Them that asks no questions isn't told a lie —
Watch the wall, my darling, while the Gentlemen go by!

THE COASTWISE LIGHTS

*Our brows are bound with spindrift and the weed is on
    our knees;*
*Our loins are battered 'neath us by the swinging,
    smoking seas.*
*From reef and rock and skerry — over headland, ness, and
    voe —*
*The Coastwise Lights of England watch the ships of
    England go!*

*Through the endless summer evenings, on the lineless,
    level floors;*
*Through the yelling Channel tempest when the siren
    hoots and roars —*
*By day the dipping house-flag and by night the rocket's
    trail —*
*As the sheep that graze behind us so we know them
    where they hail.*

We bridge across the dark, and bid the helmsman have a
care,
The flash that, wheeling inland, wakes his sleeping wife
to prayer.
From our vexed eyries, head to gale, we bind in burning
chains
The lover from the sea-rim drawn – his love in English
lanes.

We greet the clippers wing-and-wing that race the
Southern wool;
We warn the crawling cargo-tanks of Bremen, Leith, and
Hull;
To each and all our equal lamp at peril of the sea –
The white wall-sided warships or the whalers of Dundee!

Come up, come in from Eastward, from the guardports of
the Morn!
Beat up, beat in from Southerly, O gipsies of the Horn!
Swift shuttles of an Empire's loom that weave us main to
main,
The Coastwise Lights of England give you welcome back
again!

Go, get you gone up-Channel with the sea-crust on your
  plates;
Go, get you into London with the burden of your
  freights!
Haste, for they talk of Empire there, and say, if any
  seek,
The Lights of England sent you and by silence shall ye
  speak!

THE LOWESTOFT BOAT

(*East Coast Patrols of the War*)

1914–18

In Lowestoft a boat was laid,
    Mark well what I do say!
And she was built for the herring-trade,
    But she has gone a-rovin', a-rovin', a-rovin'
    The Lord knows where!

They gave her Government coal to burn,
And a Q.F. gun at bow and stern,
And sent her out a-rovin',etc.

Her skipper was mate of a bucko ship
Which always killed one man per trip,
So he is used to rovin', etc.

Her mate was skipper of a chapel in Wales,
And so he fights in topper and tails –
Religi-ous tho' rovin', etc.

Her engineer is fifty-eight,
So he's prepared to meet his fate,
Which ain't unlikely rovin', etc.

Her leading-stoker's seventeen,
So he don't know what the Judgments mean,
Unless he cops 'em rovin', etc.

Her cook was chef in the Lost Dogs' Home,
*   Mark well what I do say!*
And I'm sorry for Fritz when they all come
*   A-rovin', a-rovin', a-roarin' and a-rovin',*
*   Round the North Sea rovin',*
*   The Lord knows where!*

BIG STEAMERS

1914-18

"Oh, where are you going to, all you Big Steamers,
  With England's own coal, up and down the salt
  seas?"
"We are going to fetch you your bread and your butter,
  Your beef, pork, and mutton, eggs, apples, and
  cheese."

"And where will you fetch it from, all you Big Steamers,
  And where shall I write you when you are away?"
"We fetch it from Melbourne, Quebec, and Vancouver –
  Address us at Hobart, Hong-Kong, and Bombay."

But if anything happened to all you Big Steamers,
  And suppose you were wrecked up and down the salt
  sea?"
"Then you'd have no coffee or bacon for breakfast,
  And you'd have no muffins or toast for your tea."

"Then I'll pray for fine weather for all you Big Steamers,
For little blue billows and breezes so soft."
"Oh, billows and breezes don't bother Big Steamers,
For we're iron below and steel-rigging aloft."

"Then I'll build a new lighthouse for all you Big
Steamers,
With plenty wise pilots to pilot you through."
Oh, the Channel's as bright as a ball-room already,
And pilots are thicker than pilchards at Looe."

"Then what can I do for you, all you Big Steamers,
Oh, what can I do for your comfort and good?"
"Send out your big warships to watch your big waters,
That no one may stop us from bringing you food.

"For the bread that you eat and the biscuits you
nibble,
The sweets that you suck and the joints that you
carve,
They are brought to you daily by all us Big
Steamers —
And if any one hinders our coming you'll
starve!"

'THE TRADE'

(Sea Warfare)

1914–18

They bear, in place of classic names,
  Letters and numbers on their skin.
They play their grisly blindfold games
  In little boxes made of tin.
    Sometimes they stalk the Zeppelin,
Sometimes they learn where mines are laid,
  Or where the Baltic ice is thin.
That is the custom of 'The Trade'.

Few prize-courts sit upon their claims.
  They seldom tow their targets in.
They follow certain secret aims
  Down under, far from strife or din.
    When they are ready to begin
No flag is flown, no fuss is made
  More than the shearing of a pin.
That is the custom of 'The Trade'.

The Scout's quadruple funnel flames
   A mark from Sweden to the Swin,
The Cruiser's thund'rous screw proclaims
   Her comings out and goings in:
   But only whiffs of paraffin
Or creamy rings that fizz and fade
   Show where the one-eyed Death has been.
That is the custom of 'The Trade'.

Their feats, their fortunes and their fames
   Are hidden from their nearest kin;
No eager public backs or blames,
   No journal prints the yarn they spin
   (The Censor would not let it in!)
When they return from run or raid.
   Unheard they work, unseen they win.
That is the custom of 'The Trade'.

THE HOLY WAR

1917

A tinker out of Bedford,
  A vagrant oft in quod,
A private under Fairfax,
  A minister of God –
Two hundred years and thirty
  Ere Armageddon came
His single hand portrayed it,
  And Bunyan was his name!

He mapped for those who follow,
  The world in which we are –
'This famous town of Mansoul'
  That takes the Holy War.
Her true and traitor people,
  The Gates along her wall,
From Eye Gate unto Feel Gate,
  John Bunyan showed them all.

All enemy divisions,
  Recruits of every class,
And highly screened positions
  For flame or poison-gas;
The craft that we call modern,
  The crimes that we call new,
John Bunyan had 'em typed and filed
  In Sixteen Eighty-two.

Likewise the Lords of Looseness
  That hamper faith and works,
The Perseverance-Doubters,
  And Present-Comfort shirks,
With brittle intellectuals
  Who crack beneath a strain —
John Bunyan met that helpful set
  In Charles the Second's reign

Emmanuel's vanguard dying
  For right and not for rights,
My Lord Apollyon lying
  To the State-kept Stockholmites,

The Pope, the swithering Neutrals,
  The Kaiser and his Gott —
Their rôles, their goals, their naked souls —
  He knew and drew the lot.

Now he hath left his quarters,
  In Bunhill fields to lie,
The wisdom that he taught us
  Is proven prophecy —
One watchword through our Armies,
  One answer from our lands: —
"No dealings with Diabolus
  As long as Mansoul stands!"

A pedlar from a hovel,
  The lowest of the low —
The Father of the Novel,
  Salvation's first Defoe —
Eight blinded generations
  Ere Armageddon came,
He showed us how to meet it,
  And Bunyan was his name!

THE CHILDREN

("The Honours of War" – *A Diversity of Creatures*)

1914–18

*These were our children who died for our lands: they were
    dear in our sight.*
    *We have only the memory left of their home-treasured
        sayings and laughter.*
    *The price of our loss shall be paid to our hands, not
        another's hereafter.*
*Neither the Alien nor Priest shall decide on it. That is
    our right.*
        But who shall return us the children?

*At the hour the Barbarian chose to disclose his pretences,
    And raged against Man, they engaged, on the breasts
        that they bared for us,
    The first felon-stroke of the sword he had long-time
        prepared for us –
Their bodies were all our defence while we wrought our
    defences.*

They bought us anew with their blood, forbearing to
    blame us,
Those hours which we had not made good when the
    Judgment o'ercame us.
They believed us and perished for it. Our statecraft, our
    learning
Delivered them bound to the Pit and alive to the burning
Whither they mirthfully hastened as jostling for honour –
Not since her birth has our Earth seen such worth loosed
    upon her.

Nor was their agony brief, or once only imposed on them.
    The wounded, the war-spent, the sick received no
    exemption:
Being cured they returned and endured and achieved our
    redemption,
Hopeless themselves of relief, till Death, marvelling,
    closed on them.

*That flesh we had nursed from the first in all cleanness
    was given*
*To corruption unveiled and assailed by the malice of
    Heaven —*
*By the heart-shaking jests of Decay where it lolled on the
    wires —*
*To be blanched or gay-painted by fumes — to be cindered
    by fires —*
To be senselessly tossed and retossed in stale mutilation
From crater to crater. For this we shall take expiation.
    But who shall return us our children?

M.I.

(Mounted Infantry of the Line)

*I wish my mother could see me now, with a fence-post
    under my arm,*
*And a knife and a spoon in my putties that I found on a
    Boer farm,*
*Atop of a sore-backed Argentine, with a thirst that you
    couldn't buy.*
    I used to be in the Yorkshires once
    (Sussex, Lincolns, and Rifles once),
    Hampshires, Glosters, and Scottish Once! (ad lib.)
        But now I am M.I.

*That is what we are known as — that is the name you
    must call*
*If you want officers' servants, pickets an' 'orseguards an'
    all —*
Details for buryin'-parties, company-cooks or supply —
Turn out the chronic Ikonas! Roll up the ——[1] M.I.!

[1] Number according to taste and service of audience.

My 'ands are spotty with veldt-sores, my shirt is a button
    an' frill,
An' the things I've used my bay'nit for would make a
    tinker ill!
An' I don't know whose dam' column I'm in, nor where
    we're trekkin' nor why.
    I've trekked from the Vaal to the Orange once –
    From the Vaal to the greasy Pongolo once –
    (Or else it was called the Zambesi once) –
        For now I am M.I.

That is what we are known as – we are the push you
    require
For outposts all night under freezin', an' rearguard all day
    under fire.
Anything 'ot or unwholesome? Anything dusty or dry?
Borrow a bunch of Ikonas! Trot out the —— M.I.!

Our Sergeant-Major's a subaltern, our Captain's a
    Fusilier –
Our Adjutant's "late of Somebody's 'Orse," an' a
    Melbourne auctioneer;
But you couldn't spot us at 'arf a mile from the crackest
    caval-ry.

They used to talk about Lancers once,
Hussars, Dragoons, an' Lancers once,
'Elmets, pistols, an' carbines once,
    But now we are M.I.!

That is what we are known as — we are the orphans they
    blame
For beggin' the loan of an 'ead-stall an' makin' a mount
    to the same.
'Can't even look at their 'orselines but some one goes
    bellerin' "Hi!
"'Ere comes a burglin' Ikona! Footsack, you —— M.I.!"

We're trekkin' our twenty miles a day an' bein' loved by
    the Dutch,
But we don't hold on by the mane no more, nor lose our
    stirrups — much;
An' we scout with a senior man in charge where they 'oly
    white flags fly.
    We used to think they were friendly once,
    Didn't take any precautions once
    (Once, my ducky, an' only once!)
        But now we are M.I.!

116

That is what we are known as — we are the beggars that
   got
Three days "to learn equitation," an' six month o'
   bloomin' well trot!
Cow-guns, an' cattle, an' convoys — an' Mister De Wet
   on the fly —
We are the rollin Ikonas! We are the —— M.I.

The new fat regiments come from home, imaginin' vain
   V.C.'s
(The same as your talky-fighty men which are often
   Number Threes[1]),
But our words o' command are "Scatter" an' "Close" an'
   "Let your wounded lie."
   We used to rescue 'em noble once, —
   Givin' the range as we raised 'em once —
   Getting' 'em killed as we saved 'em once —
      But now we are M.I.

---

[1] Horse-holders when in action and therefore generally under
   cover

That is what we are known as — we are the lanterns you
     view
After a fight round the kopjes, lookin' for men that we
     knew;
Whistlin' an' callin' together, 'altin' to catch the reply:-
"'Elp me! O 'elp me, Ikonas! This way, the —— M.I.!"

I wish my mother could see me now, a-gatherin' news on
     my own,
When I ride like a General up to the scrub and ride back
     like Tod Sloan,
Remarkable close to my 'orse's neck to let the shots go by.
     We used to fancy it risky once
     (Called it a reconnaissance once),
     Under the charge of an orf'cer once,
          But now we are M.I.!

That is what we are known as — that is the song you must
     say
When you want men to be Mausered at one and a penny a
     day;
We are no five-bob Colonials — we are the 'ome-made
     supply,
Ask for the London Ikonas! Ring up the —— M.I.!

I wish myself could talk to myself as I left 'im a year ago;
I could tell 'im a lot that would save 'im a lot on the
    things that 'e ought to know!
When I think o' that ignorant barrack-bird, it almost
    makes me cry
  I used to belong in an Army once
  (Gawd! what a rum little Army once),
  Red little, dead little Army once!
      But now I am M.I.!

That is what we are known as — we are the men that
  have been
Over a year at the business, smelt it an' felt it an' seen.
We 'ave got 'old of the needful — you *will* be told by
  and by;
Wait till you've 'eard the Ikonas, spoke to the old M.I.!

Mount — march, Ikonas! Stand to your 'orses again!
Mop off the frost on the saddles, mop up the miles
  on the plain.
Out go the stars in the dawnin', up goes our dust
  to the sky,
Walk — trot, Ikonas! Trek jou[1] the old M.I.!

[1] Get ahead.

"Soldier an' Sailor Too"

(The Royal Regiment of Marines)

As I was spittin' into the Ditch aboard o' the *Crocodile*,
I seed a man on a man-o'-war got up in the Reg'lars' style.
'E was scrapin' the paint from off of 'er plates, an' I sez to
   'im, "'Oo are you?"
Sez 'e, "I'm a Jolly — 'Er Majesty's Jolly — soldier an'
   sailor too!'
Now 'is work begins by Gawd knows when, and 'is work is
   never through;
'E isn't one o' the reg'lar Line, nor 'e isn't one of the crew.
'E's a kind of a giddy harumfrodite — soldier an' sailor too!

An', after, I met 'im all over the world, a-doin' all kinds of
   things,
Like landin' 'isself with a Gatlin' gun to talk to them
   'eathen kings;
'E sleeps in an 'ammick instead of a cot, an' 'e drills with
   the deck on a slew,
An' 'e sweats like a Jolly — 'Er Majesty's Jolly — soldier
   an' sailor too!

For there isn't a job on the top o' the earth the beggar
    don't know, nor do —
You can leave 'im at night on a bald man's 'ead, to
    paddle 'is own canoe —
'E's a sort of a bloomin' cosmopolouse — soldier an' sailor
    too.

We've fought 'em in trooper, we've fought 'em in dock,
    and drunk with 'em in betweens,
When they called us the seasick scull'ry-maids, an' we
    called 'em the Ass-Marines;
But, when we was down for a double fatigue, from
    Woolwich to Bernardmyo,
We sent for the Jollies — 'Er Majesty's Jollies — soldier
    an' sailor too!
They think for 'emselves, an' they steal for 'emselves,
    and they never ask what's to do,
But they're camped an' fed an' they're up an' fed before
    our bugle's blew.
Ho! they ain't no limpin' procrastitutes — soldier an'
    sailor too.

You may say we are fond of an 'arness-cut, or 'ootin' in
*   barrick-yards,*
Or startin' a Board School mutiny along o' the Onion
*   Guards;* [1]
But once in a while we can finish in style for the ends of
*   the earth to view,*
The same as the Jollies — 'Er Majesty's Jollies — soldier
*   an' sailor too!*
They come of our lot, they was brothers to us; they was
*   beggars we'd met an' knew;*
Yes, barrin' an inch in the chest an' the arm, they was
*   doubles o' me an' you;*
For they weren't no special chrysanthemums — soldier an'
*   sailor too!*

To take your chance in the thick of a rush, with firing all
*   about,*
Is nothing so bad when you've cover to 'and, an' leave
*   an' likin' to shout;*
But to stand an' be still to the Birken'ead drill[2] *is a*
*   damn' tough bullet to chew,*

[1] Long ago a battalion of Guards sent to Bermuda for
notorious conduct in barracks.
[2] When the Birkenhead was sunk off Simon's Bay (1852) the
Marines aboard went down as drawn up on her deck.

122

An' they done it, the Jollies − 'Er Majesty's Jollies −
    soldier an' sailor too!
Their work was done when it 'adn't begun; they was
    younger nor me an' you;
Their choice it was plain between drownin' in 'eaps an'
    bein' mopped by the screw,
So they stood an' was still to the Birken'ead *drill,*
    soldier an' sailor too!

We're most of us liars, we're 'arf of us thieves, an' the
    rest are as rank as can be,
But once in a while we can finish in style (which I 'ope it
    won't 'appen to me).
But it makes you think better o' you an' your friends,
    an' the work you may 'ave to do,
When you think o' the sinkin' Victorier's *Jollies −*
    soldier an' sailor too!
Now there isn't no room for to say ye don't know − they
    'ave proved it plain and true −
That, whether it's Widow, *or whether it's ship,*
    Victorier's *work is to do,*
An' they done it, the Jollies − 'Er Majesty's jollies −
    soldier an' sailor too!

SAPPERS

(Royal Engineers)

When the Waters were dried an' the Earth did appear,
("It's all one," says the Sapper),
The Lord He created the Engineer,
*   Her Majesty's Royal Engineer,*
*   With the rank and pay of a Sapper!*

When the Flood come along for an extra monsoon,
'Twas Noah constructed the first pontoon
*   To the plans of Her Majesty's, etc.*

But after fatigue in the wet an' the sun,
Old Noah got drunk, which he wouldn't ha' done
*   If he'd trained with, etc.*

When the Tower o' Babel had mixed up men's bat,[1]
Some clever civilian was managing that,
An' none of, etc.

---

[1] Talk.

When the Jews had a fight at the foot of a hill,
Young Joshua ordered the sun to stand still,
   For he was a Captain of Engineers, *etc.*

When the Children of Israel made bricks without straw,
They were learnin' the regular work of our Corps,
   The work of, *etc.*

For ever since then, if a war they would wage,
Behold us a-shinin' on history's page –
   First page for, *etc.*

We lay down their sidings an' help 'em entrain,
An' we sweep up their mess through the blooming'
    campaign
   In the style of, *etc.*

They send us in front with a fuse an' a mine
To blow up the gates that are rushed by the Line,
   But bent by, *etc.*

They send us behind with a pick an' a spade,
To dig for the guns of a bullock-brigade
  Which has asked for, etc.

We work under escort in trousers and shirt,
An' the heathen they plug us tail-up in the dirt,
  Annoying, etc.

We blast out the rock an' we shovel the mud,
We make 'em good roads an' — they roll down the
  khud,[2]
  Reporting, etc.

We make 'em their bridges, their wells, an' their huts,
An' the telegraph-wire the enemy cuts,
  An' it's blamed on, etc.

An' when we return, an' from war we would cease,
They grudge us adornin' the billets of peace,
  Which are kept for, etc.

---

[2] Hillside.

We build 'em nice barracks — they swear they are bad,
That our Colonels are Methodist, married or mad,
  Insultin', etc.

They haven't no manners nor gratitude too,
For the more that we help 'em, the less will they do,
  But mock at, etc.

Now the Line's but a man with a gun in his hand,
An' Cavalry's only what horses can stand,
  When helped by, etc.

Artillery moves by the leave o' the ground,
But we are the men that do something all round,
  For we are, etc.

I have stated it plain, an' my argument's thus
  ("It's all one," says the Sapper)
There's only one Corps which is perfect — that's us;
  An' they call us Her Majesty's Engineers,
  Her Majesty's Royal Engineers,
  With the rank and pay of a Sapper!

UBIQUE

(Royal Artillery)

There is a word you often see, pronounce it as you may —
"You bike," "you bykwee," "Ubbikwe" — alludin' to
  R.A.
It serves 'Orse, Field, an' Garrison as motto for a crest;
An' when you've found out all it means I'll tell you 'alf
  the rest.

Ubique means the long-range Krupp be'ind the low-range
  'ill —
Ubique means you'll pick up an', while you do, stand
  still.
Ubique means you've caught the flash an' timed it by the
  sound.
Ubique means five gunners' 'ash before you've loosed a
  round.

Ubique means Blue Fuse,[1] an' make the 'ole to sink the
   trail.
Ubique means stand up an' take the Mauser's 'alf-mile
   'ail.
Ubique means the crazy team not God nor man can 'old.
Ubique means that 'orse's scream which turns your
   innards cold!

Ubique means "Bank, 'Olborn, Bank — a penny all the
   way" —
The soothin', jingle-bump-an'-clank from day to
   peaceful day.
Ubique means "They've caught De Wet, an' now we
   shan't be long."
Ubique means "I much regret, the beggar's goin' strong!"

Ubique means the tearin' drift where, breech-blocks
   jammed with mud,
The khaki muzzles duck an' lift across the khaki flood.
Ubique means the dancing plain that changes rocks to
   Boers.
Ubique means mirage again an' shellin' all outdoors.

---

[1] Extreme range.

129

Ubique means "Entrain at once for Grootdefeatfontein."
Ubique means "Off-load your guns" – at midnight in the rain!
Ubique means "More mounted men. Return all guns to store."
Ubique means the R.A.M.R. Infantillery Corps. [1]

Ubique means that warnin' grunt the perished linesman knows,
When o'er 'is strung an' sufferin' front the shrapnel sprays 'is foes;
An' as their firin' dies away the 'usky whisper runs
From lips that 'aven't drunk all day: "The Guns! Thank Gawd, the Guns!"

Extreme, depressed, point-blank or short, end-first or any'ow,
From Colesberg Kop to Quagga's Poort – from Ninety-Nine till now –
By what I've 'eard the others tell an' I in spots 'ave seen,
There's nothin' this side 'Eaven or 'Ell Ubique doesn't mean!

[1] The Royal Artillery Mounted Rifles – when mounted infantry were badly needed.

"THE SERVICE MAN"

(Prelude to "Service Songs" in *The Five Nations*)

"Tommy" you was when it began,
  But now that it is o'er
You shall be called The Service Man
  'Enceforward, evermore.

Batt'ry, brigade, flank, centre, van,
  Defaulter, Army-corps —
From first to last, The Service Man
  'Enceforward, evermore.

From 'Alifax to 'Industan,
  From York to Singapore —
'Orse, foot, an' guns, The Service Man
  'Enceforward, evermore!

THE RETURN

Peace is declared, an' I return
*   To 'Ackneystadt, but not the same;*
Things 'ave transpired which made me learn
*   The size and meanin' of the game.*
I did no more than others did,
*   I don't know where the change began.*
I started as a average kid,
*   I finished as a thinkin' man.*

If England was what England seems,
    An' not the England of our dreams,
But only putty, brass, an' paint,
    'Ow quick we'd drop 'er! *But she ain't!*

132

Before my gappin' mouth could speak
    I 'eard it in my comrade's tone.
I saw it on my neighbour's cheek
    Before I felt it flush my own.
An' last it come to me – not pride,
    Nor yet conceit, but on the 'ole
(If such a term may be applied),
    The makin's of a bloomin' soul.

Rivers at night that cluck an' jeer,
    Plains which the moonshine turns to sea,
Mountains which never let you near,
    An' stars to all eternity;
An' the quick-breathin' dark that fills
    The 'ollows of the wilderness,
When the wind worries through the 'ills –
    These may 'ave taught me more or less.

Towns without people, ten times took,
    An' ten times left an' burned at last;
An' starvin' dogs that come to look
    For owners when a column passed;
An' quiet, 'omesick talks between
    Men, met by night, you never knew
Until — 'is face — by shellfire seen —
    Once — an struck off. They taught me too.

The day's lay-out — the mornin' sun
    Beneath your 'at-brim as you sight;
The dinner-'ush from noon till one,
    An' the full roar that lasts till night;
An' the pore dead that look so old
    An' was so young an hour ago,
An' legs tied down before they're cold —
    These are the things which make you know.

Also Time runnin' into years —
  A thousand Places left be'ind —
An' Men from both two 'emispheres
  Discussin' things of every kind;
So much more near than I 'ad known,
  So much more great than I 'ad guessed —
An' me, like all the rest, alone —
  But reachin' out to all the rest!

So 'ath it come to me — not pride,
  Nor yet conceit, but on the 'ole
(If such a term may be applied),
  The makin's of a bloomin' soul.
But now, discharged, I fall away
  To do with little things again …
Gawd, 'oo knows all I cannot say,
  Look after me in Thamesfontein![1]

If England was what England seems,
  An' not the England of our dreams,
But only putty, brass, an' paint,
  'Ow quick we'd chuck 'er! *But she ain't!*

[1] London.

135

PARADE-SONG OF THE CAMP-ANIMALS

("Her Majesty's Servants" – *The Jungle Book*)

ELEPHANTS OF THE GUN-TEAMS

We lent to Alexander the strength of Hercules,
The wisdom of our foreheads, the cunning of our knees.
We bowed our necks to service – they ne'er were loosed
   again, –
Make way there, way for the ten-foot teams
     Of the Forty-Pounder train!

GUN-BULLOCKS

Those heroes in their harnesses avoid a cannon-ball,
And what they know of powder upsets them one and all;
Then we come into action and tug the guns again, –
Make way there, way for the twenty yoke
     Of the Forty-Pounder train!

CAVALRY HORSES

By the brand on my withers, the finest of tunes
Is played by the Lancers, Hussars, and Dragoons,
And it's sweeter than "Stables" or "Water" to me,
The Cavalry Canter of "Bonnie Dundee!"

Then feed us and break us and handle and groom,
And give us good riders and plenty of room,
And launch us in column of squadron and see
The Way of the War-horse to "Bonnie Dundee!"

SCREW-GUN MULES

As me and my companions were scrambling up a hill,
The path was lost in rolling stones, but we went forward
    still;
For we can wriggle and climb, my lads, and turn up
    every-where,
And it's our delight on a mountain height, with a leg or
    two to spare!

Good luck to every sergeant, then, that lets us pick our
    road!
Bad luck to all the driver-men that cannot pack a load!
For we can wriggle and climb, my lads, and turn up
    every-where,
And it's our delight on a mountain height, with a leg or
    two to spare!

We haven't a camelty tune of our own
To help us trollop along,
But every neck is a hair-trombone
(Rtt–ta–ta–ta! is a hair-trombone!)
And this is our marching-song:
Can't! Don't! Shan't! Won't!
Pass it along the line!
Somebody's pack has slid from his back,
'Wish it were only mine!
Somebody's load has tipped off in the road –
Cheer for a halt and a row!
Urr! Yarrh! Grr! Arrh!
Somebody's catching it now!

ALL THE BEASTS TOGETHER

Children of the Camp are we,
Serving each in his degree;
Children of the yoke and goad,
Pack and harness, pad and load.
See our line across the plain,
Like a heel-rope bent again,
Reaching, writhing, rolling far,
Sweeping all away to war!
While the men that walk beside,
Dusty, silent, heavy-eyed,
Cannot tell why we or they
March and suffer day by day.

   Children of the Camp are we,
   Serving each in his degree;
   Children of the yoke and goad,
   Pack and harness, pad and load!

CAIN AND ABEL

Western Version
1934

Cain and Abel were brothers born.
   (Koop-la! Come along, cows!)
One raised cattle and one raised corn.
   (Koop-la! Come along! Co-hoe!)

And Cain he farmed by the river-side,
So he did not care how much it dried.

For he banked, and he sluiced, and he ditched and he led
   (And the Corn don't care for the Horn) –
A-half Euphrates out of her bed
   To water his dam' Corn!

But Abel herded out on the plains
Where you have to go by the dams and the rains.

It happened, after a three-year drought,
The wells, and the springs, and the dams gave out.

The Herd-bulls came to Cain's new house
　　(They wanted water so! —)
With the hot red Sun between their brows,
Sayin' "Give us water for our pore cows!"
　　But Cain he told 'em — "No!"

The Cows they came to Cain's big house
With the cold white Moon between their brows,
Sayin' "Give some water to us pore cows!"
　　But Cain he told 'em — "No!"

The li'l Calves came to Cain's fine house
With the Evenin' Star between their brows,
Sayin' "give us water an' we'll be cows!"
　　But Cain he told 'em — "No!"

The Herd-bulls led 'em back again,
An' Abel went an' said to Cain:—
"Oh, sell me water, my brother dear,
Or there will be no beef this year."
　　And Cain he answered — "No!"

"Then draw your hatches, my brother true,
An' let a little water through."
　　But Cain he answered: - "No!

"My dams are tight an' my ditches are sound,
An' not a drop goes through or round
　　Till she's done her duty by the Corn.

"I will not sell, an' I will not draw,
An' if you breach, I'll have the Law,
　　As sure as you are born!"

Then Abel took his best bull-goad,
An' holed a dyke on the Eden road.

He opened her up with foot an' hand,
An' let Euphrates loose on the land.

He spilled Euphrates out on the plain,
So's all his cattle could drink again.

Then Cain he saw what Abel done –
But, in those days, there was no Gun!

So he made him a club of a hickory-limb,
An' halted Abel an' said to him: —

"I did not sell an' I did not draw,
An' now you've breached I'll have the Law.

'You ride abroad in your hat an' spurs,
Hell-hoofin' over my cucumbers!

"You pray to the Lord to send you luck
An' you loose your steers in my garden-truck:

"An' now you're bust, as you ought to be,
You can keep on prayin' but not to me!"

Then Abel saw it meant the life;
But, in those days, there was no Knife:

So he up with his big bull-goad instead,
But — Cain hit first and dropped him dead!

The Herd-bulls ran when they smelt the blood,
An' horned an' pawed in that Red Mud.
The Calves they bawled, and the Steers they milled,
Because it was the First Man Killed;
An' the whole Herd broke for the Land of Nod,
An' Cain was left to be judged by God!

But seein' all he had had to bear,
I never could call the Judgment fair!